HOW TO CREATE JAZZ CHORD PROGRESSIONS

by Chuck Marohnic

TABLE OF CONTENTS

THE CYCLE OF FIFTHS

It can be said that all or most of our music, that is of the Western world, is based on the cycle of fifths using the Ionian Mode (C to C). A thorough knowledge of the cycle is not only helpful but essential for the professional musician in today's world of musical demands.

Let us begin with a simple diagram of the cycle.

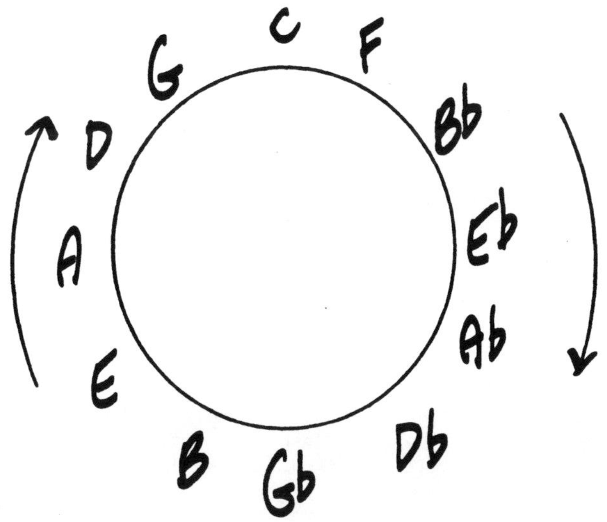

You will notice the direction of the arrows. THE DIRECTION OF THE ARROWS INDICATES THE HARMONIC RESOLUTION OR SIMPLY, THE MANNER IN WHICH THE CHORDS MOVE. For example; D goes to G, G goes to C, or E♭ goes to A♭, A♭ moves to D♭. Thus by a simple study of the above diagram, you can understand the movement of the cycle in any key.

EX 1. Fill in the blanks.

A goes to ___	G goes to ___
C goes to ___	F goes to ___
B♭ goes to ___	B goes to ___

THE II-V-I-PROGRESSION

This progression is the substance of which most music in the western world is made. While most music theory courses offer a reasonable approach to this subject, they often leave the student with merely an academic understanding rather than a working one.

Let us refer to the cycle of fifths again. In the previous exercise, you saw that D goes to G, etc. We will now try to establish a key to work in. Let us begin with the key of F. As you notice on the diagram, F is preceded by C. If our tonal center or tonic is F, then we must look backward to C to see that it moves to F. What is important here is to remember the direction in which we are moving, or where we are going. We are coming home, as it were, to the key of F. We now take that C and make it a dominant 7th or C7. C7 is the fifth of F and therefore resolves to F. In order to complete our II-V-I progression, we now have to find what it is that moves to C. Again we look backward from C and we discover G. We now make our G minor because the key of F has one flat, B♭. The progression has now become Gm to C7 to F. The II-V-I progression in the key of F is now complete. Gm = II, C7 = V7, and F = I.

Let us now try the following exercise.

EX 2.

___ goes to___that goes to F.
Dm goes to G7 that goes to___.
___goes to A7 that goes to___.
B♭ m goes to___that goes to A♭ .
___goes to___that goes to A.
F♯ m goes to___that goes to___
A♭ m goes to___that goes to___.

Practice writing and playing the II-V-I progression in all keys. You will note that you may begin at any point on the cycle and use it as your key or tonal center. Also, you may at this point think this is too elementary but it will not hurt you to review thoroughly that which you think you already know.

We have now examined the movement of the II-V-I progression in all twelve keys. At this time, you may begin to think of the I chord as either major or minor (I).

The following is an illustration of how to use the II-V-I progression:

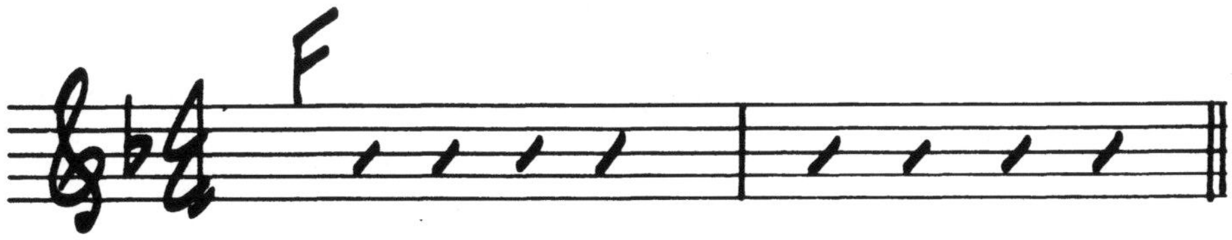

As you can plainly see, the above is at its simplest state. If we substitute our II-V for the F chord in the first measure, we end up with a much more interesting progression.

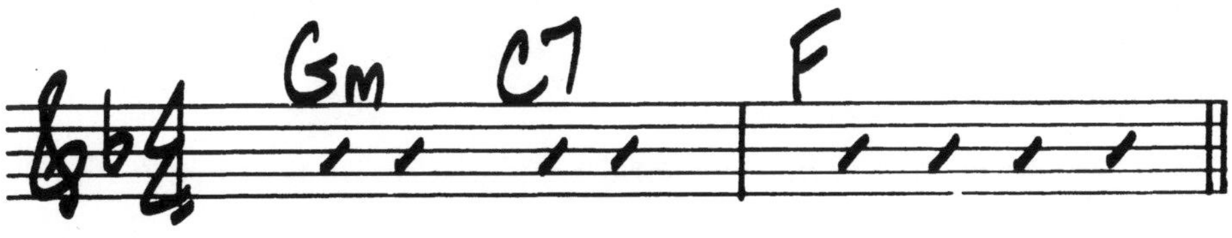

CHORD NOTATION

The following chord symbols will be used for the remainder of this book.

minor — a minus sign (-)
major 7th — a triangle (△)
minor 7, 5 or a half-diminished circle with a slash (ø)
augmented — plus sign (+)
lowered tone — (♭)
repeat sign — (%)
diminished — (o)

CHORD SUBSTITUTION

We have all been confronted with the problem of playing tunes that have simple or lousy changes or chords. This study will help you to create your own harmonic style without having to rely on someone else's changes. You will be able to read fake book or sheet music chords and add your own harmonic ideas to make the music harmonically enjoyable.

There are a number of ways to approach the problem of chord substitution. They are: cycle extension, relative majors and minors, diminished and half diminished chords, the alternate or tri-tone substitutions and finally, a combination of both cycle extension and the alternate cycle.

You will not only be able to add your own harmonic ideas but you will also be able to understand other chord progressions that seemed otherwise confusing to you.

On the preceding page, you have already begun choral substitution by using your knowledge of the cycle of fifths.

CYCLE EXTENSION

Let us begin with the following illustration:

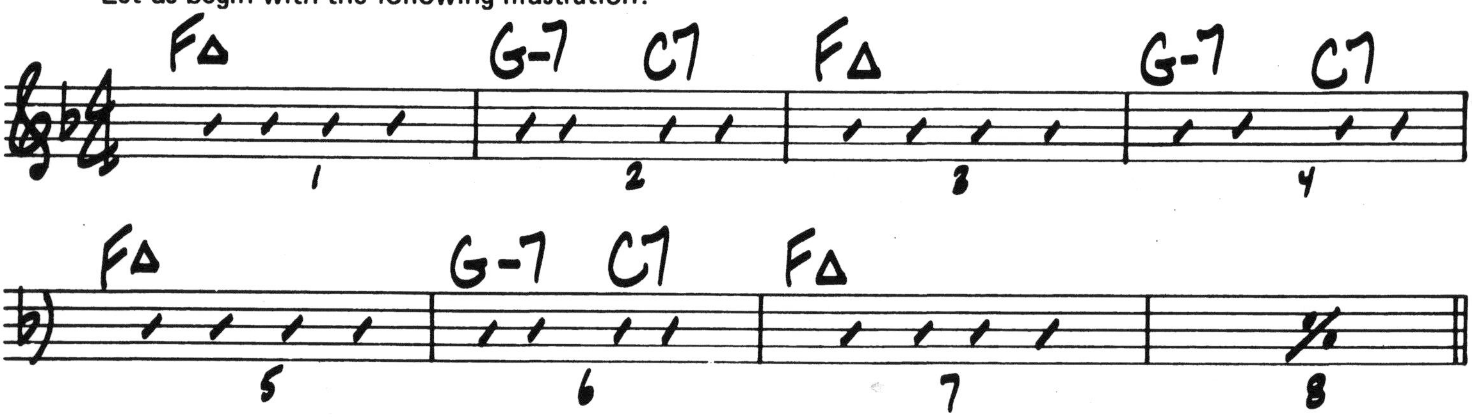

In this illustration, we see an eight bar phrase that keeps using the same II-V-I progression over and over. The question is what to do. If we refer back to the cycle of fifths, we see that Gm goes to C7 which finally resolves to F. If we allow each bar to have two chords in it, then we need something in bar 1, 3, and 5. Each of these bars has an F chord in it. Now if we think of the Gm chords in bars 2, 4, 6, as TEMPORARY ONE (I) CHORDS, then we need a chord that will resolve to Gm. After looking at the diagram of the cycle, we see that D goes to G. Therefore, if the Gm is considered a temporary I chord, we need to make the D a dominant 7 chord, because the 5 of any I is most always dominant.

We have now added a D7 to bars 1, 3, and 5. Why? Because we were concerned with the Gm chords and how to get to them smoothly. Thus we chose D7 ; D7 most always goes to Gm.

Complete the following exercise.

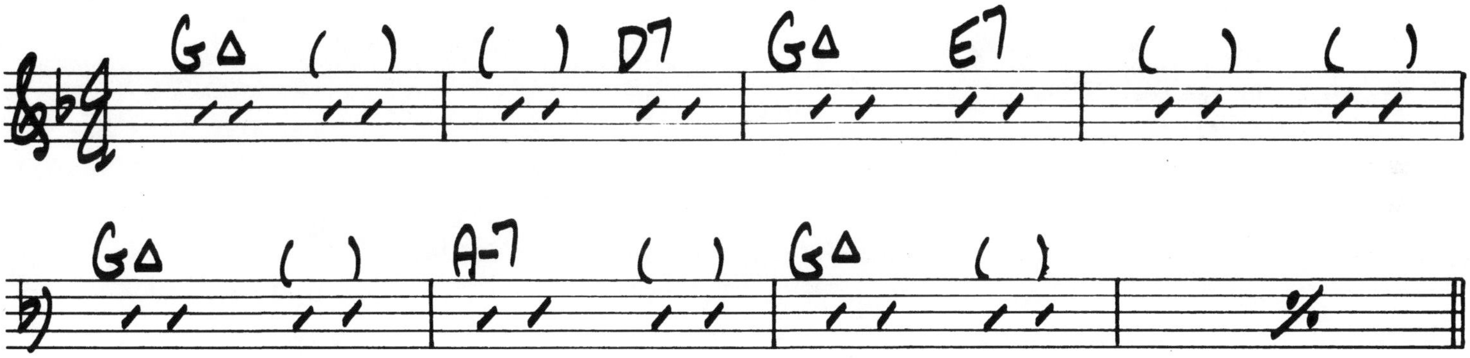

Now practice writing, transposing and playing example 1a in all twelve keys.

You are probably wondering about using these methods in measures 7 and 8. While this technique would work there, we enter into the problem of what is commonly known as turn-arounds which we will cover later in this book. So, for the time being, we will just leave these bars alone.

FURTHER CYCLE EXTENSION

EX. 2

We can now go a little further with our substitutions. Let us concentrate on bar 3 and 5. You may now consider substituting something for the F major 7 chords. We will leave the F's in bars 1, 7 and 8 alone because they represent the tonic. The exercise begins in F and ends there also. Now to bars 3 and 5.

If we go back to our cycle, we want to find something that will move smoothly to our D7. The constant of F is redundant. Now, what will go to D? Again, go backward on the cycle, because we must consider where we are going. Since we are moving to D, then we see that A goes to D. Now the question is "what kind of A do we need?" The answer is that when we consider the D7, we were thinking of the Gm as a TEMPORARY I chord. So, if we make the A an Am, we now have a II-V-I progression in Gm. Think of this in temporary terms.

Below you can see how the Am functions as a good substitute for the F chord. Now study this and play it through using all twelve keys.

EX. 2A

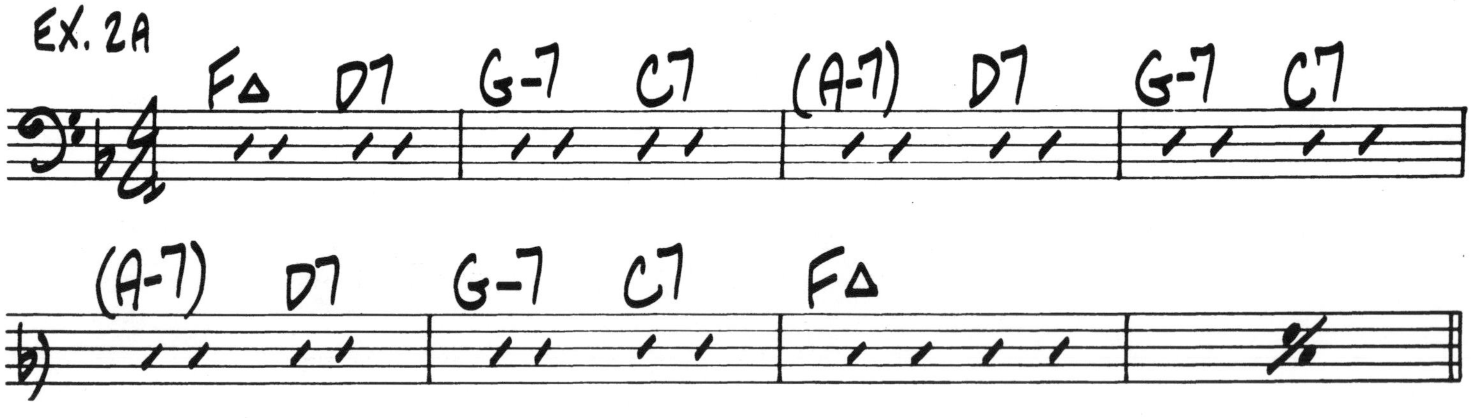

For improvisational consideration, you will notice that example 2a seems to fall into three separate phrases. The first phrase occurs in the first two measures, the second occurs in the next two bars and the third phrase occurs in the last four bars. This particular pattern makes the total eight bars rhythmically symmetrical, and also makes it easier to play. Try to think of your phrasing as it you were talking, taking pauses, etc.

The following example is from a well known standard tune.

EX. 3

Now these particular changes are okay to play. As a matter of fact, most musicians probably do play these. However, one of the great jazz trumpeters happens to prefer playing the following:

EX. 3A

You will notice that the key is A♭ and in the first bar each of the four beats has a separate chord. This example is a ballad, so it really does not seem too crowded because the tempo is very slow.

Now let's take it apart. In measure one, the only original chord is the Gm. Where did he get the C7 on beat number 4? He sees the Gm as a II7 of the Fm. Therefore, he completes the II-V-I progression in Fm by adding the C7 which is the V of Fm. He then takes the Gm and treats it temporarily as a I chord and then puts the appropriate II-V in front of it to make a II-V-I progression in Gm.

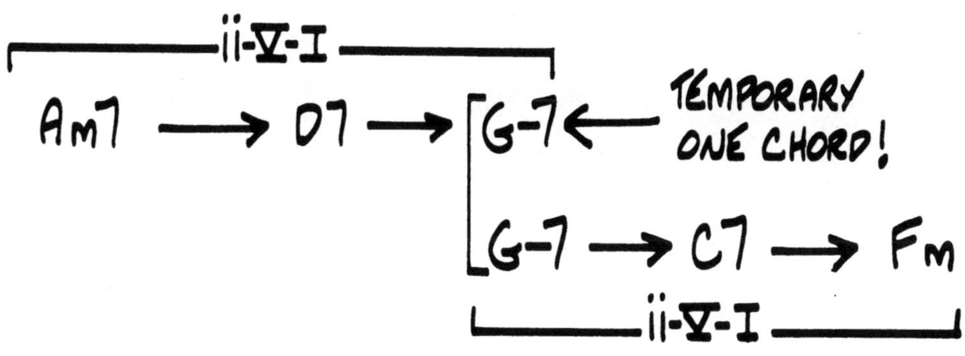

If this seems a little confusing to you, go back to examples 2 and 2a. Remember the cycle of fifths and the direction in which you are going. D goes to G, and A goes to D, etc.

You should now try to find examples of the I-V-II progression in tunes you already know and in music that you already have.

Here's another example of a well known standard.

EX. 4

Now in this example there are many different ways you can alter the harmony for improvisation. The manner in which you make your changes is determined by the phrasing you select and of course the melody. Since there is no melody here, we will just think in terms of phrases.

Let's assume that you select two separate phrases, the first four bars and the second four bars. In the first four bars, if we consider bar number two, then we need something to go to what cord? Gm! The Gm in the third bar is what we have to look at. So we'll think of that Gm as temporary I chord and put in the necessary chords to complete the II-V-I in Gm. It then looks like this:

EX. 4A

The second four bars can be treated in a similar fashion.

EX 4B

At this point I have taken the liberty of moving the C7 over a little to make room for another chord. We still retain the C7 but now we have a little more space in which to work. Again, look back to our cycle of fifths and find the necessary chord that will go to C7. It is the Gm of course. Now what will go to Gm? D7!! You may be wondering about the original Gm and why I didn't do something with that. You can if you wish, but you don't have to because the phrase will sound fine as it is. Here is the finished product. Now study this closely and play through it a few times.

EXAMPLE 4b completed.

EX. 4C (4A+B)

On the following page you will find a series of exercises to complete. Please study these thoroughly and play and write them in all twelve keys.

EXERCISES

EX. #4

EX. #5 (NOTE THE REPEAT SIGNS)

EX. #6 (NOTE: THIS IS A 12 BAR **BLUES** PROGRESSION)

ALSO NOTE THE REPEATS!

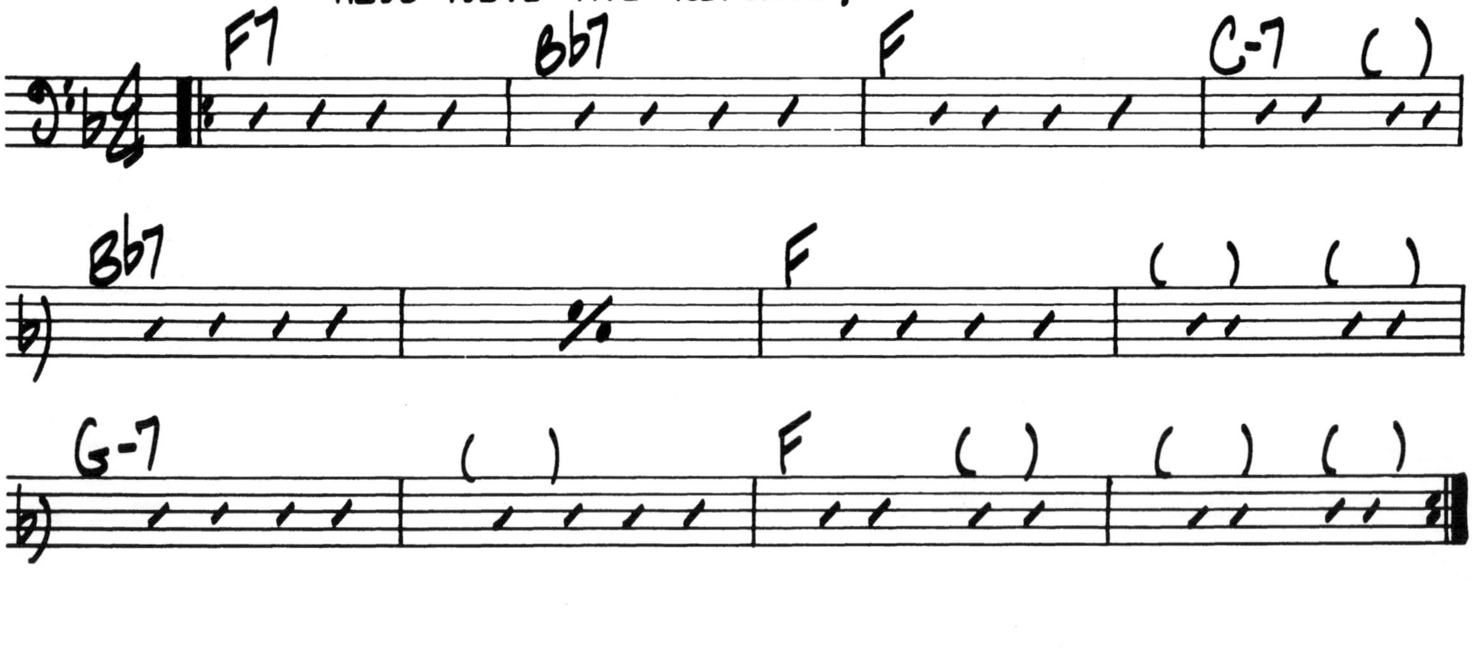

EX. #4 EXPLAINED

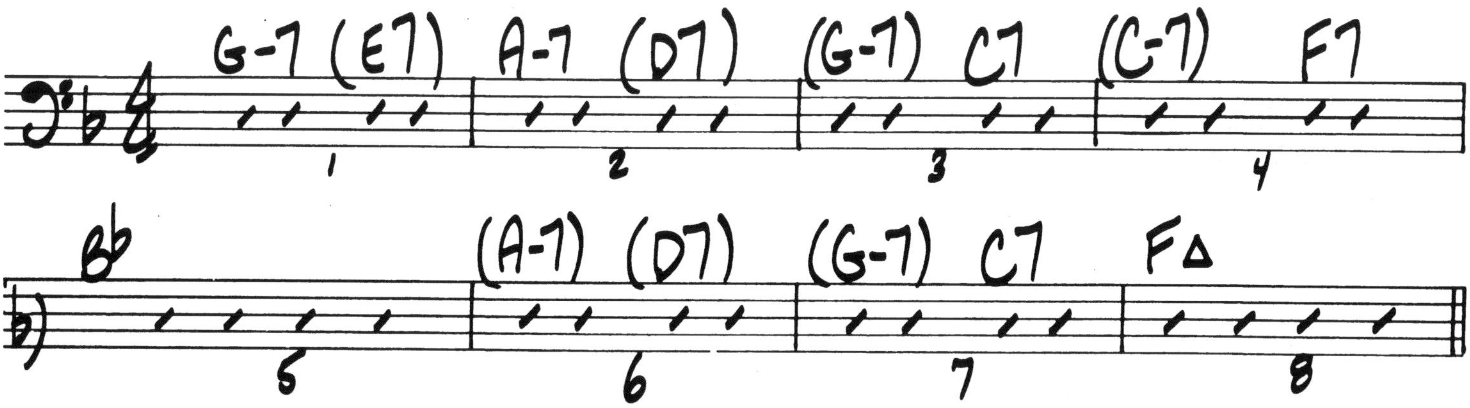

BAR NO. 1 – the E7 is the V of Am

BAR NO. 2 – determined first by bar No. 3. The Gm is the II chord of the C7. (Note: even though the Gm to C7 does not resolve to F, we try to think of the F as being understood). Now the D7 in bar No. 2 is the V of the Gm. Remember, we need to think of the cycle and not totally completing it. In other words, you must think of little groups of II-V and II-V-I.

BAR NO. 4 – the Cm is the II of II-V-I in B♭ . Remember, we are going to B♭ .

BAR NO. 6 – determined by bar No. 7. Here we have a similar situation as in bars 2 and 3. The Gm is the II of the II-V-I in F. Now we can deal with bar 6. The Am and D7 are the II and V, respectfully, of the Gm.

You can now begin to see how we can use the cycle as II-V of II-V, etc. Therefore, in easier terms, the Am in Bar No. 6 cycles out to F.

EX. #5 EXPLAINED

BAR NO. 2 – Where are you going? To the Dm in bar No. 3, therefore the Em and A7 are the II-V of the Dm.

BAR NO. 3 – first determined by bar No. 4 which figures out to be the II-V of B♭ . Therefore, in order to extend our cycle back into bar No. 3, we see that the G7 naturally goes to the Cm7 in the next bar.

BAR NO. 6 – B♭ 7 is the II7 of the V chord E♭ 7 of A♭ which, although not stated, is understood.

BAR NO. 8 – You were told to pay attention to the repeat signs. Since the piece repeats, then the Gm and C7 are the II-V of F in the first bar. If you got this one, congratulations. This will introduce you to the problem of <u>TURN-AROUNDS</u>. This will be covered next just after the explanation of Exercise No. 6.

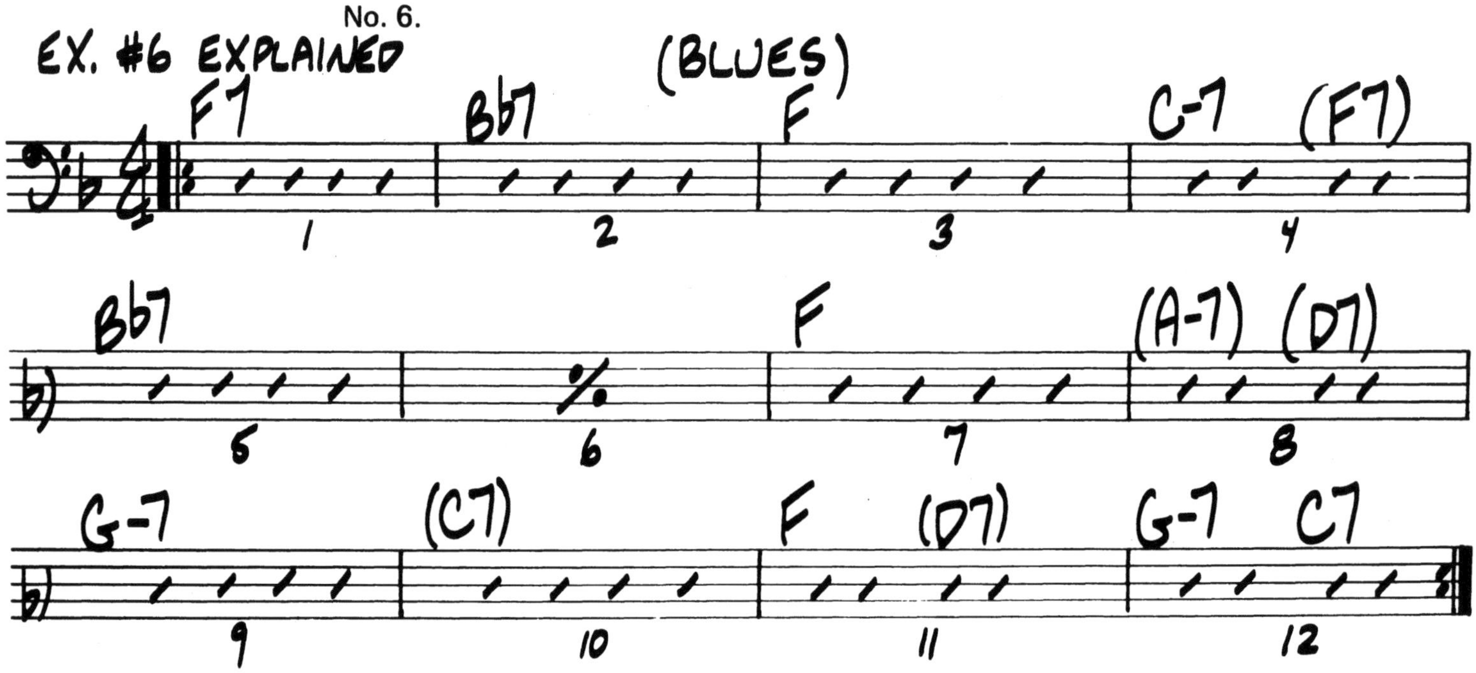

BAR NO. 4 – The F7 is the V of the II-V-I in B♭ (bar No. 5).

BAR NO. 8 – II7 and V7 respectfully of Gm in bar No. 9.

BAR NO. 10 – C 7 is the V chord of F in bar No. 11. Note that the Gm7 in bar No. 9 serves two purposes. It acts as a temporary one chord for the II-V progression in bar No. 8 and also acts as a II7 chord for the II-V-I progression in F.

BAR NO. 11 – D7 is the V7 of Gm in bar No. 12.

BAR NO. 12 – Note that again we are conceneed with the repeat signs. Therefore, Gm and C7 are the II and V7 of F in the first measure, because we are going back to BAR NO. 1. This is another example of TURN-AROUND.

TURN-AROUNDS

You have already seen a couple of examples of turn-arounds in the previous exercises. The general function of a turn-around is to turn you around, as it were, and redirect you to a place in a piece of music that you have already played. It therefore makes a repeat a much smoother move because your job in constructing a turn-around is to create a smooth harmonic resolution.

The following are the two possible ways we can construct a turn-around with the harmonic knowledge we have already acquired.

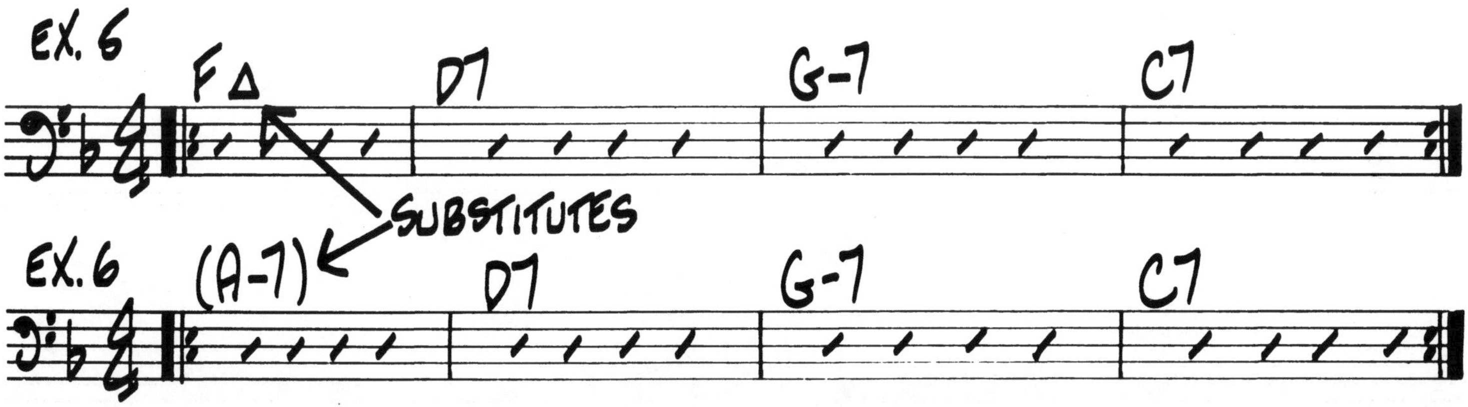

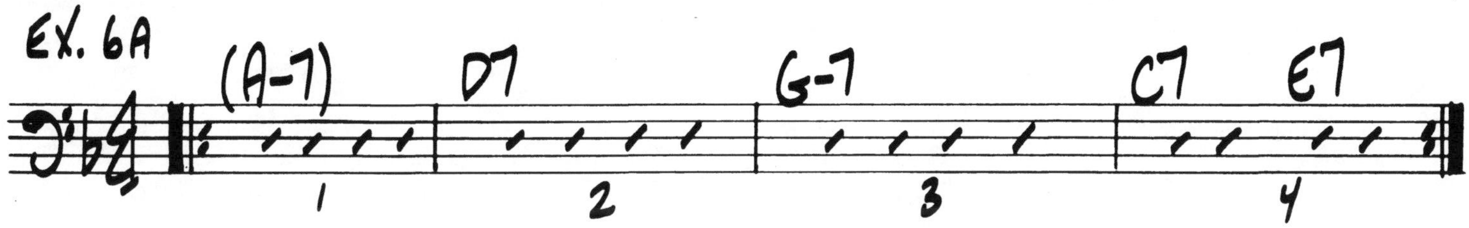

The Am in bar No. 1 is a substitute for the F in bar No. 1 of exercise No. 5. Note that in this above exercise, we have added an E7 in bar No. 4. The reason for this is that we have an option to state the E7 as a V chord of the Am in bar No. 1, or we can leave it out, thus making the C7 resolve to the understood chord of F. Either method you may choose will supply you with a nice smooth turn-around. It may be apparent to you by now that the importance of stating the one chord is somewhat flexible.

Note that you also have certain rhythmic freedom in the construction of your turn-arounds. See the following examples:

EX. 7

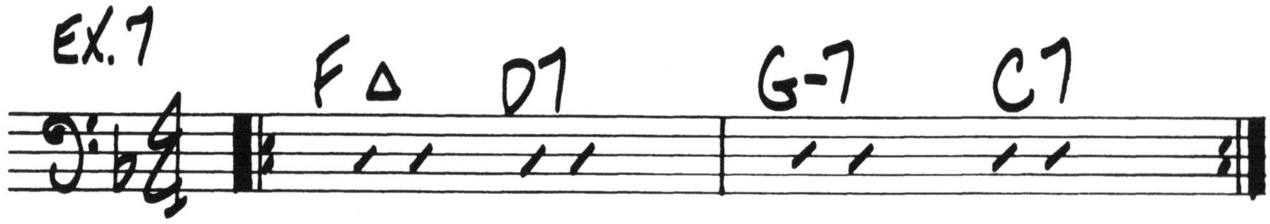

EX. 8

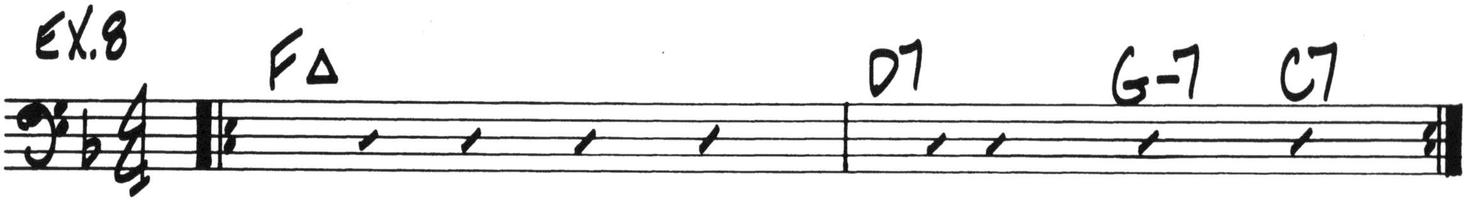

EX. 9

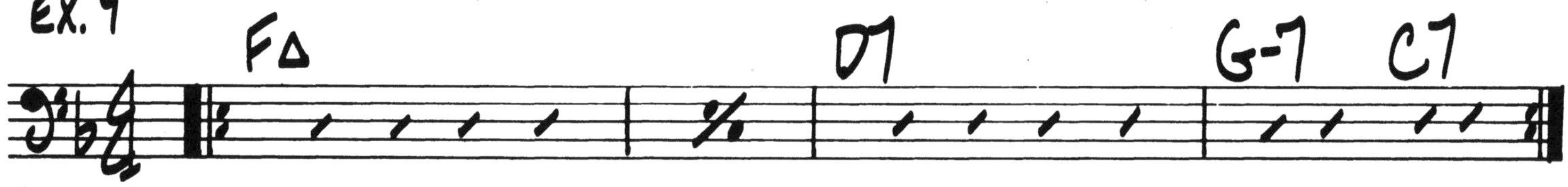

EX. 10

NOTE THAT SUBSTITUTES ARE USED IN THE ABOVE

EX. 11

EX. 12

RELATIVE MAJORS AND MINORS

BELOW ARE THE MINORS THAT CAN BE USED AS SUBSTITUTES FOR YOUR MAJORS.

C & Am – NO FLATS OR SHARPS
F & Dm – 1 FLAT
B♭ & Gm – 2 FLATS
E♭ & Cm – 3 FLATS
A♭ & Fm – 4 FLATS
D &B m – 5 FLATS
G♭ & E♭ m (F♯ & D♯ m) – 6 FLATS OR SHARPS
B & G♯m or A♭ m – 5 SHARPS
E & C m or D m – 4 SHARPS
A & F♯ m or G♭ m – 3 SHARPS
D & Bm – 2 SHARPS
G & Em – 1 SHARP

YOU NOTICE ALSO THAT THE KEY SIGNATURE OF THE MAJOR IS THE SAME AS THAT OF THE RELATIVE MINOR.

OBSERVE THE FOLLOWING EXAMPLE.

EX. 13

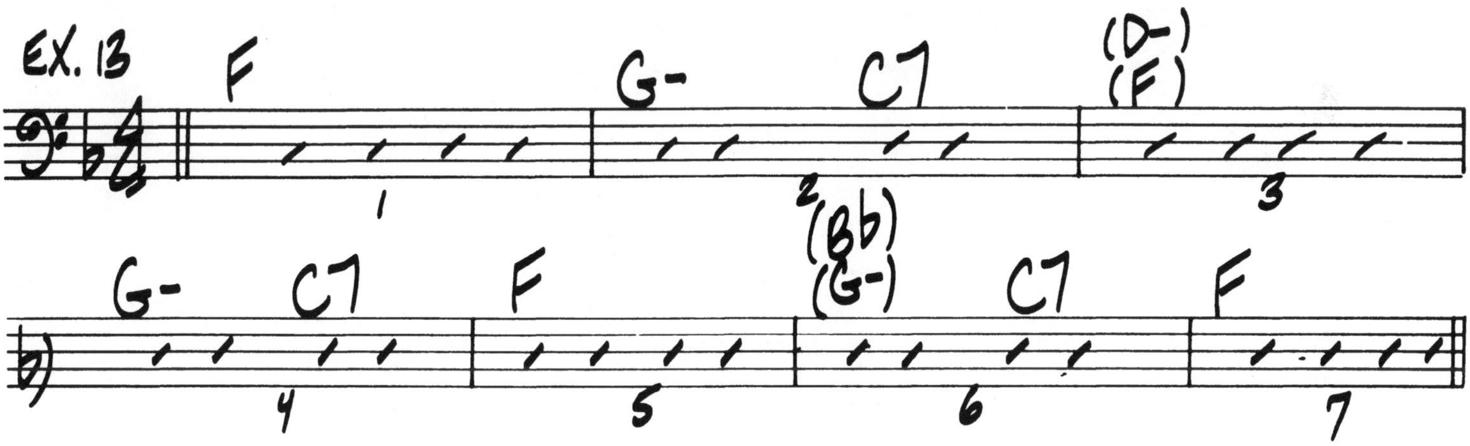

In example No. 13, we see that we can substitute the Dm in bar No. 3 for the F major and also in bar No. 6, we have selected the B♭ major as a substitute for the Gm. This technique of substitution is not the best or most frequently used, however it is another device for you to consider when altering the harmony of a tune.

The following is an example of a few bars of a well known jazz tune. Note the harmony and with your understanding of relatives, you can see in example No. 14 that the changes of this tune are not as difficult as they seem.

EX. 14

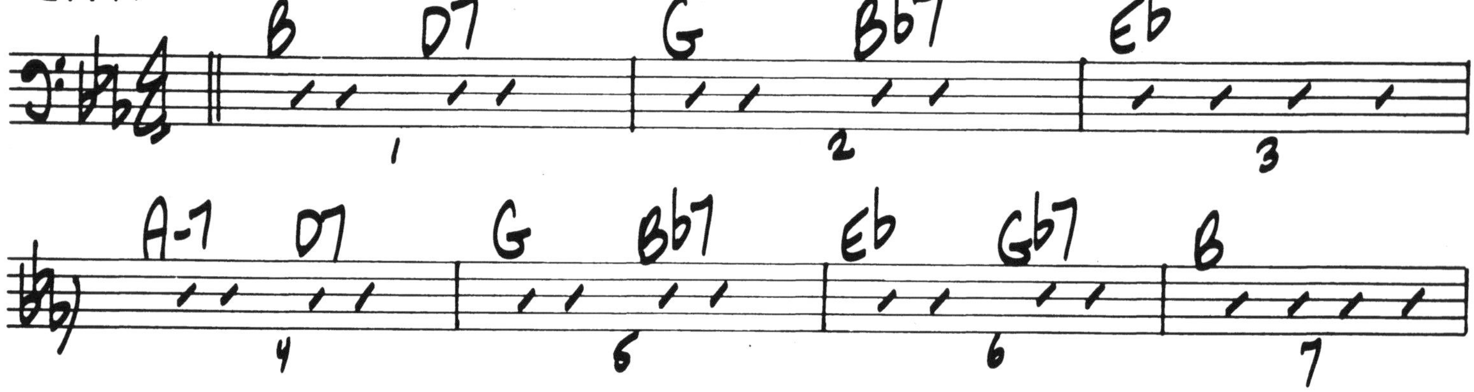

EX. 14A

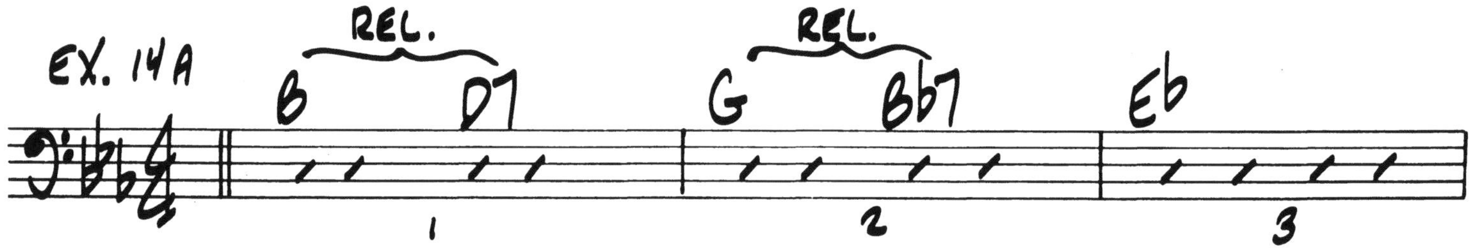

Please note in bar No. 1 how the B and D7 are related. If you examine them closely, B is the relative minor of D major. Although we do not have a B minor chord or a D major, in your linear or solo approach, you can consider this relationship. You can also see that the G and B♭ 7 in bar No. 2 are related in the same manner. B♭ major is the relative major of Gm. Therefore, in soloing, you may consider the following:

EX 14B

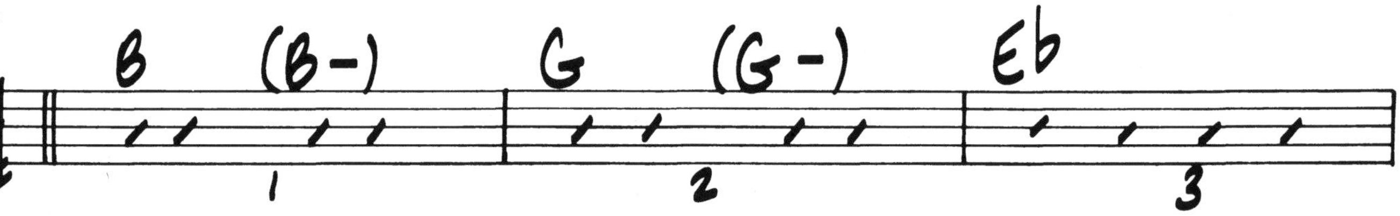

As we look at bar No. 4 in the piece, we can see the same relationship happening.

EX. 14C.

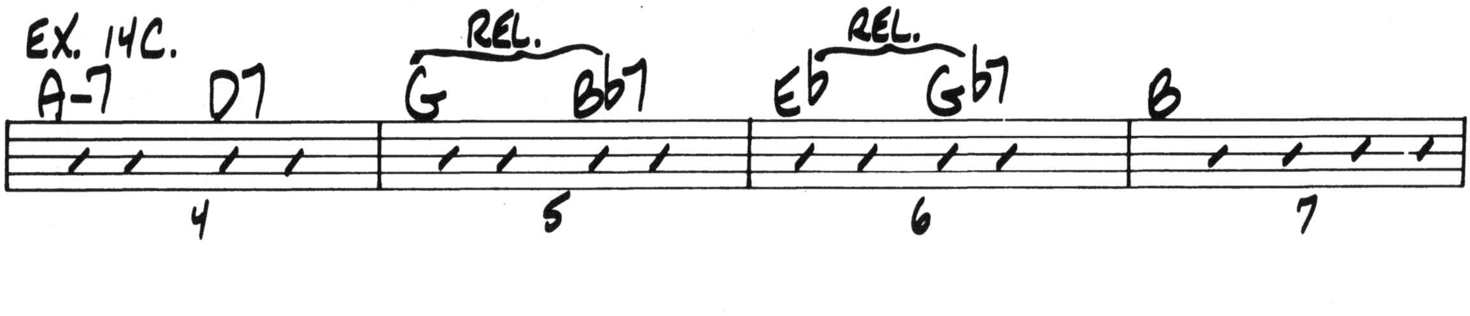

Note that the relative minor of B♭ major is Gm and the relative minor of E♭ Major is G♭ m, therefore, the bars now can become:

EX 14D.

If this confuses you, please go back and re-study the chapter on relative majors and minors. Then try to find examples of these in tunes you know and also try to use examples in harmony you already are playing.

ANALYSIS OF A WELL KNOWN TUNE

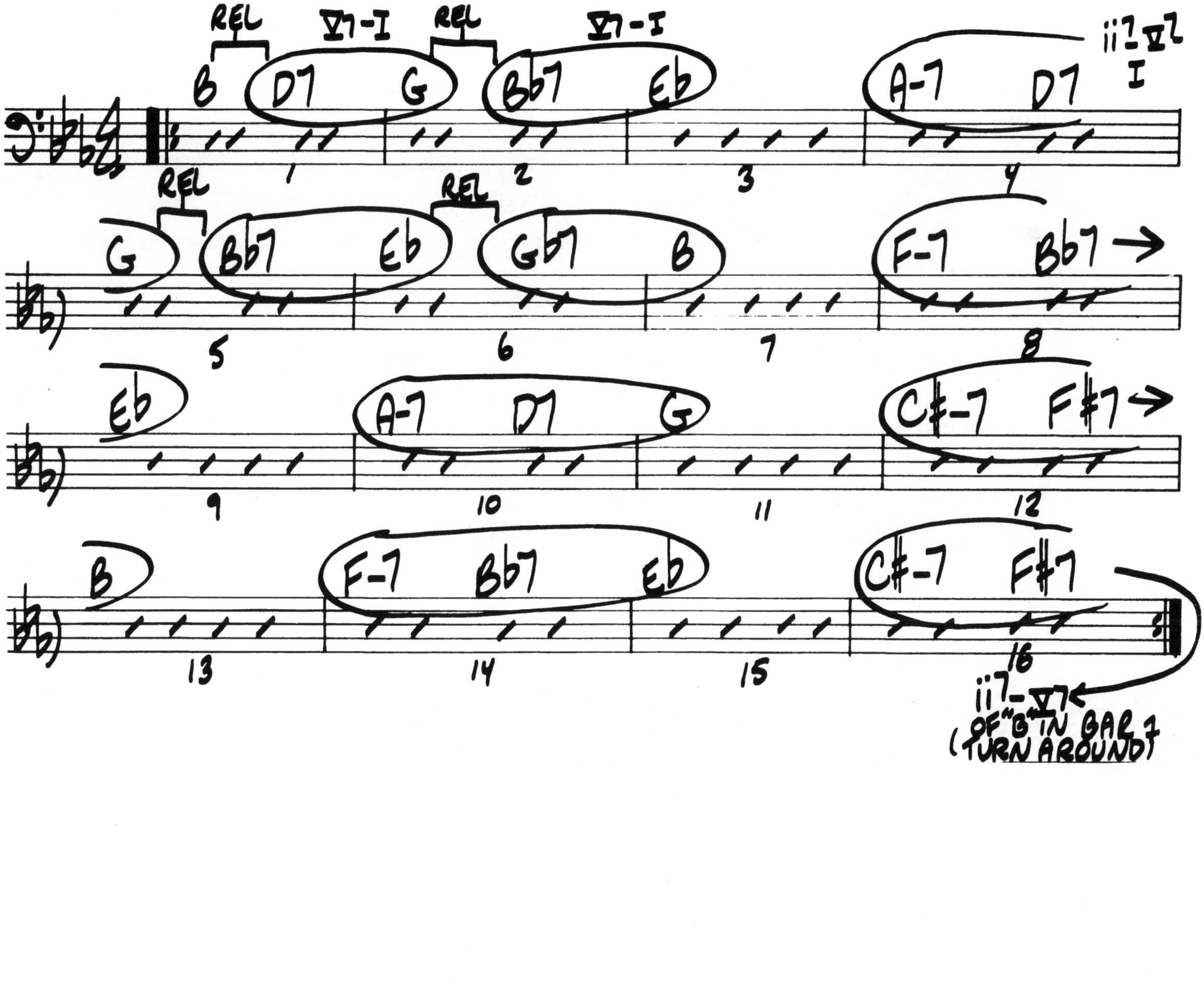

EXPLANATION OF THE ANALYSIS.

BAR NO. 1 —the B and D7 are relative to each other. (See the preceding chapter.) The D7 is also the V7 of G in the next bar.

BAR NO. 2 —G and B♭ 7 are relative to each other. B♭ 7 is the V7 of E♭ in the next bar.

BAR NO. 4 —Am7 and D7 are the II7 and V7 of G in the next bar.

BAR NO. 5 —G and B♭ 7 are relative to each other. B♭ 7 is the V7 of E♭ in the next bar.

BAR NO. 6 —E♭ and G♭ 7 are relative to each other. Also, the G♭ 7 is the V7 of B in the next bar.

BAR NO. 8 —Fm7 and B♭ 7 are the II7 and V7 of E♭ in the next bar.

BAR NO. 10— the Am7 and D7 are the II7 and V7 of G in the next bar.

BAR NO. 12 —C m7 and F 7 are the II7 and V7 of B in the next bar.

BAR NO. 14 —Fm7 and B♭ 7 are the II7 and V7 of E♭ in the next bar.

BAR NO. 12 —C♯ m7 and F♯ 7 are the II7 and V7 of B in the first bar because the repeat signs are present and therefore produce a turn-around situation.

As far as the linear approach is concerned, you can see that this tune is made up of nothing more than II7-V7-I progressions thereby constructed on the three diatonic scales of B MAJOR, E♭ MAJOR AND G MAJOR.

THE ALTERNATE CYCLE

We now come to a very important part of jazz harmony that is absolutely essential in learning how to create good and interesting chord progressions. This is the method of using the tri-tone or flat five substitutions. It will help you if you think of this method as the alternate cycle. Observe the following diagram.

EX.#7

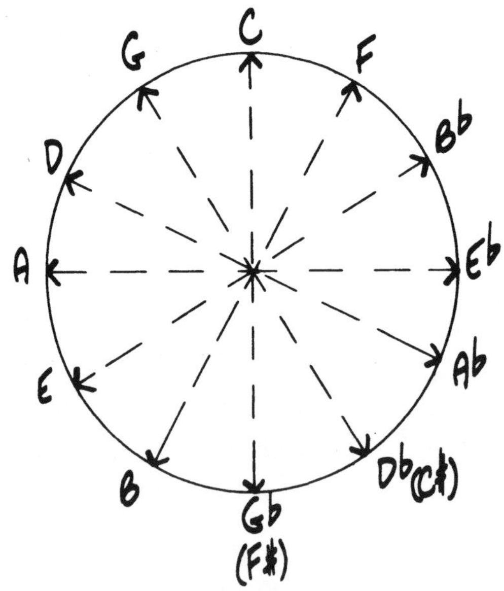

In example No. 7 we have a diagram of the cycle of fifths. However, if you notice, there are dotted lines that cut the circle on the diameter. Also you can see that the keys on one side of the circle relate to keys on the other side. How are they related? By virtue of the interval of the flatted fifth. For example, C is directly across the cycle from G♭, and they are related by the flat five or are a flat five away from each other. Therefore, the flat five of C is G♭ and vice-versa.

Now study the cycle and complete the following exercise.

EXERCISE NO. 15

C is the flat five of___	___is the ♭5 of F
B♭ is the flat five of___	___is the ♭5 of E♭
A♭ is the flat five of___	___is the ♭5 of D♭
F♯ is the flat five of___	___is the ♭5 of B
E is the flat five of___	___is the ♭5 of A
D is the flat five of___	___is the ♭5 of G

The ALTERNATE CYCLE exists in its entirety a flat five away from the CYCLE OF FIFTHS. It is almost like a mirror image of itself ... a sort of shadow. What this ultimately means is that in the case of the II-V-I progression, you have the option of using an alternate chord from the ALTERNATE CYCLE. See the following example.

EX. 8A

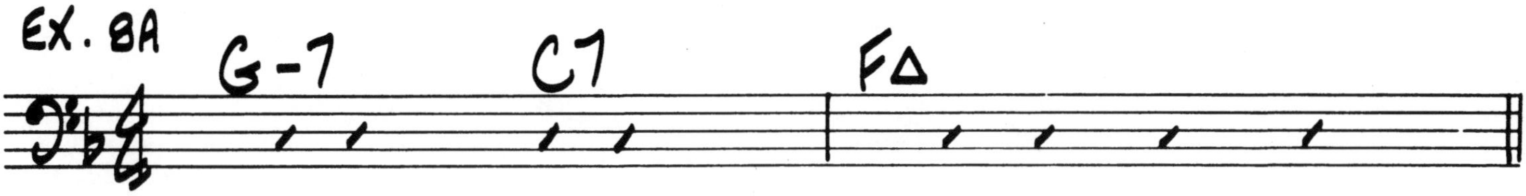

EX. 8B

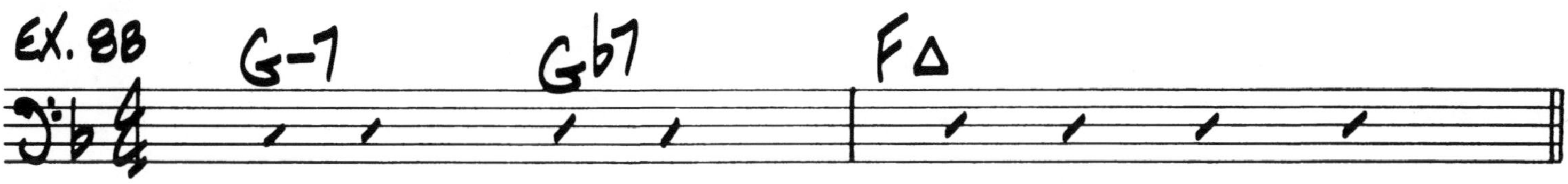

In example No. 8b we have substituted the G 7 for the ordinary C7. You remember that the G♭ is a ♭5 away from C, therefore, it may be used as an alternate chord. Also, the harmony in example 8b is chromatic. It would be advisable at this early stage to try NOT to think of the ALTERNATE CYCLE as chromatic harmony because, as you get more advanced, the chords will not always fall in a chromatic sequence.

In most instances, you will be using the alternates on the V7 chords. This does not limit you, however. You may also choose the alternate on the II7 chord, as in the following example.

EX. 9A

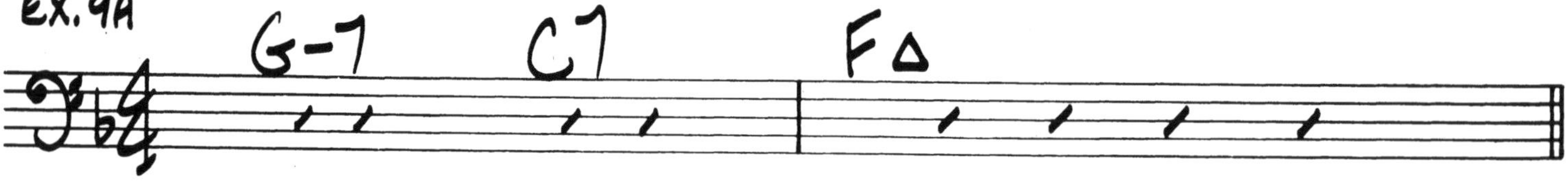

EX. 9B

You now have the option of using the alternates on either the V7, II7 or both the V7 and II7 chords as substitutes for the original progression. Now study and play this method in all twelve keys.

CYCLE EXTENSION USING THE ALTERNATES

EX. 10

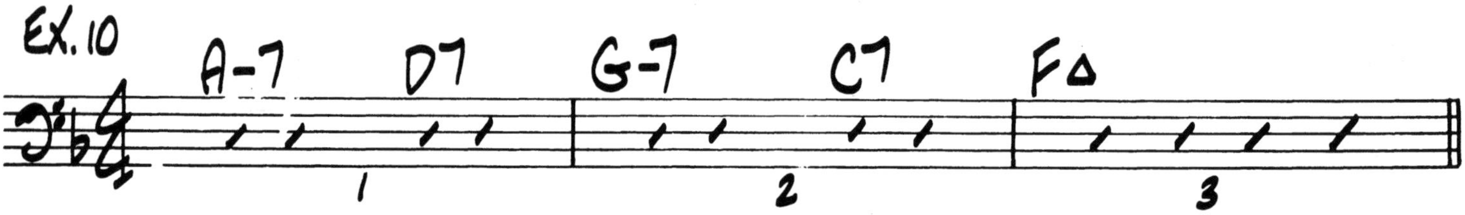

We have already dealt with the progression in bar No. 2 but you may also use the same principles in bar No. 1. The progression above now has a much larger selection of progressions from which to choose. Here are just a few.

EX 10A

EX. 10B

EX. 10C

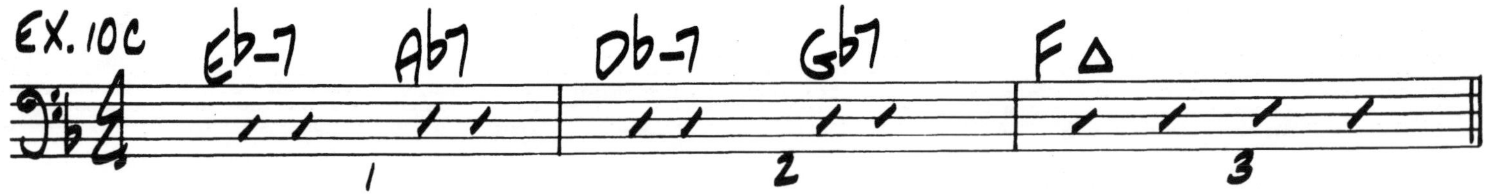

Try to analyze the selections in the above three examples and play through them; then go on to the following exercises and learn them in all twelve keys.

EXERCISES

EX. #16

EX. #17

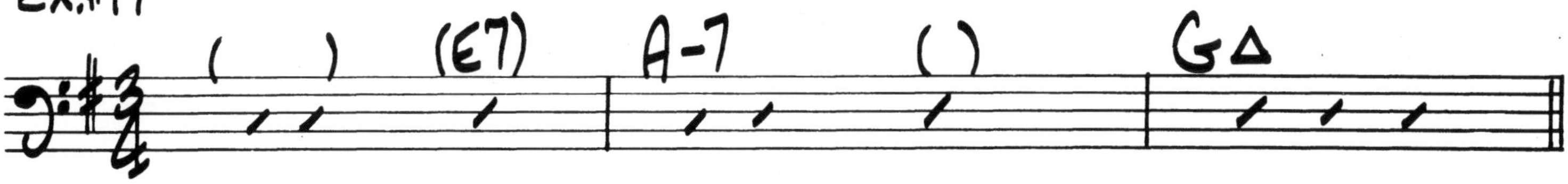

EX. #18

EXERCISE ANSWERS

EX#16

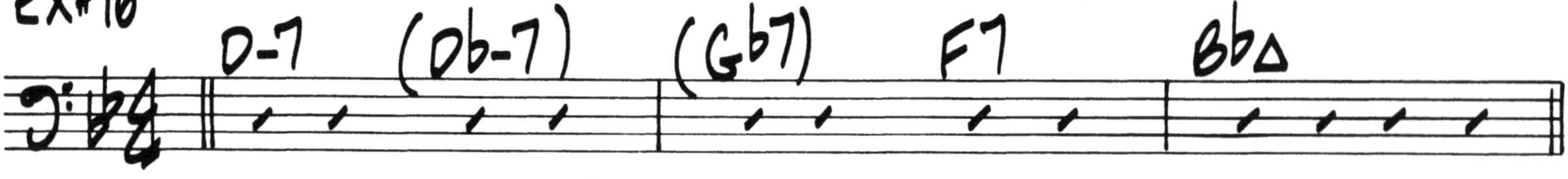

EX#17

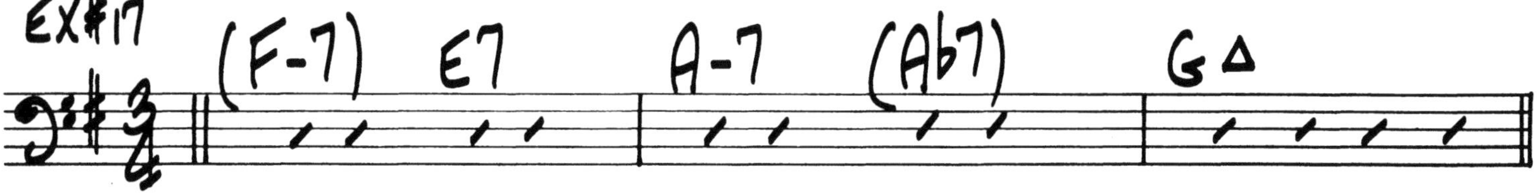

EX.#18

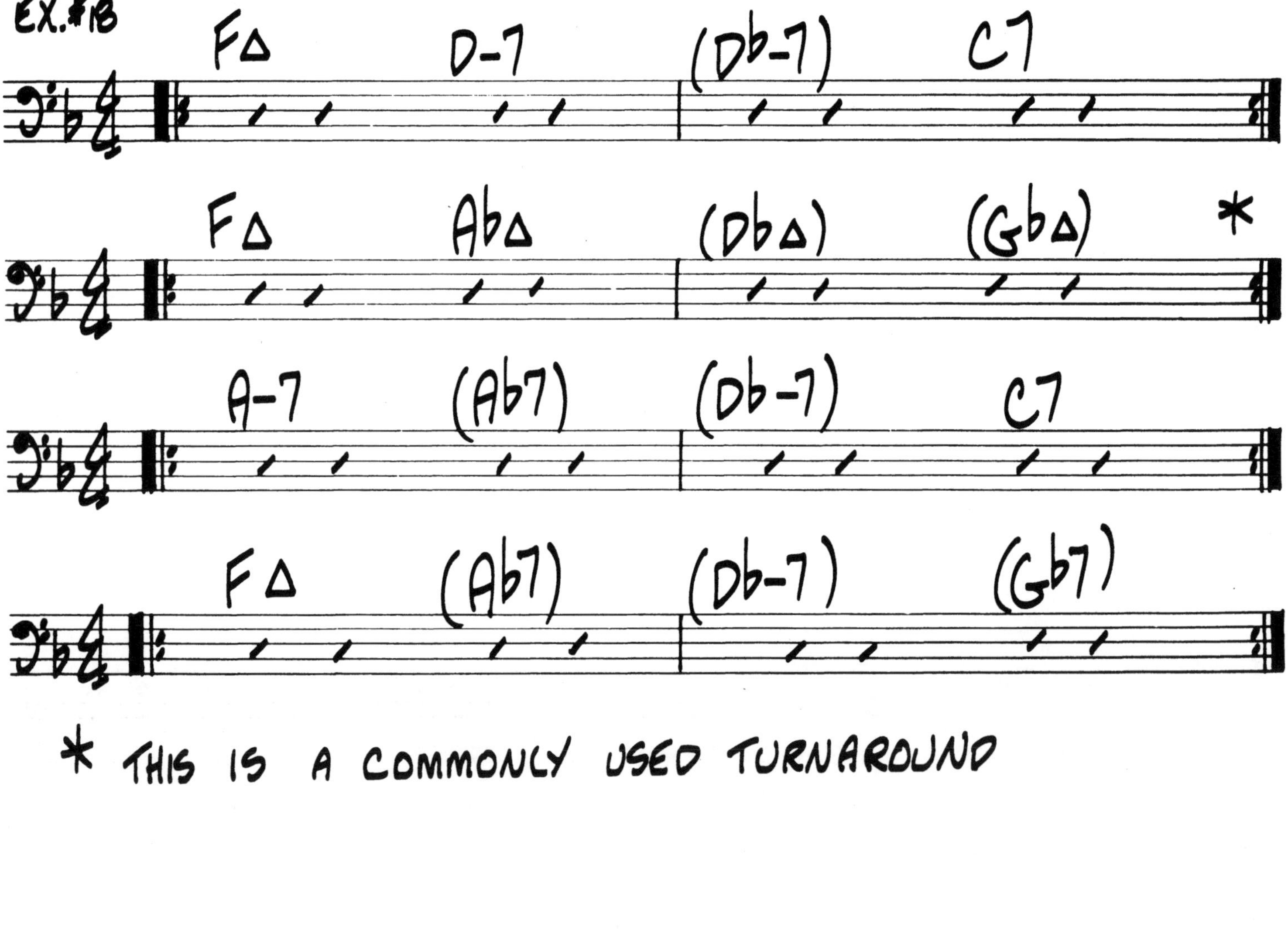

* THIS IS A COMMONLY USED TURNAROUND

Please note the following example:

EX.#11

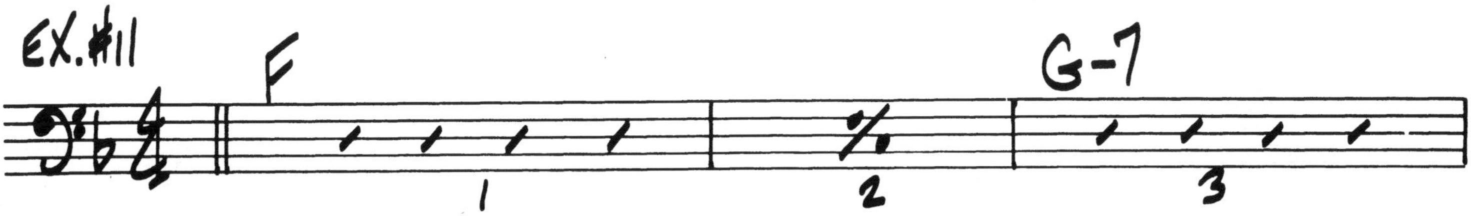

You will come across many tunes that begin with the above chord progression, the one chord leading to a II7 chord. In the example below, we have added a few chords that make up a universal jazz progression.

EX.#12

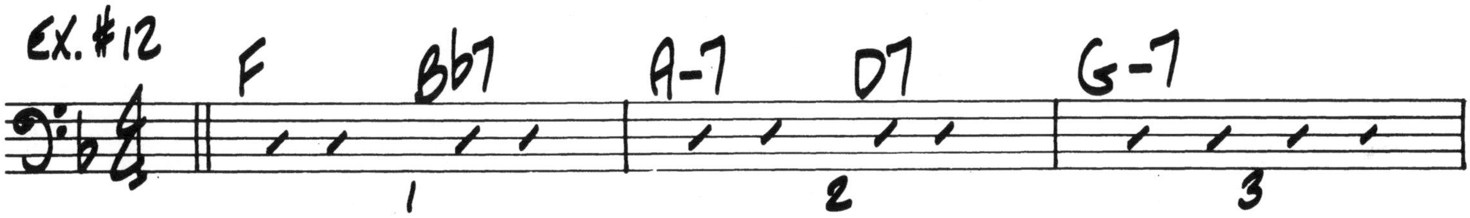

You can see readily that in measure No. 2, the Am7 and D7 are examples of extending the cycle. As for the B♭ 7 in bar No. 1, it is the alternate of E7 which would extend the cycle all the way. You may use either B♭ 7 or E7, but the B♭ 7 is the most commonly one used. A point to remember there is that this pattern can be used in different rhythms, as seen in the example below.

EX#13

EX.#14

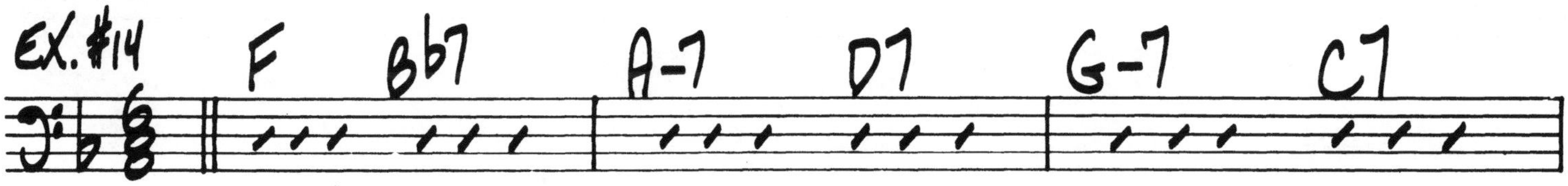

USING THE DOMINANT AND THE ALTERNATE

Now that we have learned to use the alternate, we now realize that we can use both the dominant and its alternate together. See the following:

EX#15

Here the G♭ 7 is used along with the C7. Both chords are good for resolving to the F in bar No. 1. So you now have the option of using either one or both. The use of both is a common device that bass players like to employ to give their lines a nice flowing motion. Below is a bass line that you will come across time and again.

EX. #16

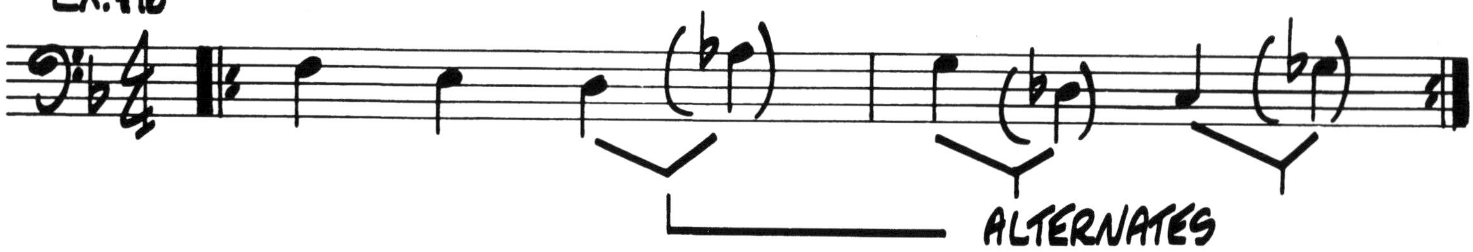

So the A♭ , D♭ , and Gb in the above are alternates used along with their ♭5 counterparts. They also serve to supply a fluid motion to the bass line by acting as leading tones. A leads to G, D♭ to C and G♭ to F.

One final note on bass lines. It will help you to be a much better player if you understand good bass line movement. Try to listen to good bass players and you will discover good solid harmony, both in selection of chords and voicings from the bottom end. The bass line is as important to good harmony as is the melody.

ANALYSIS OF A WELL KNOWN STANDARD

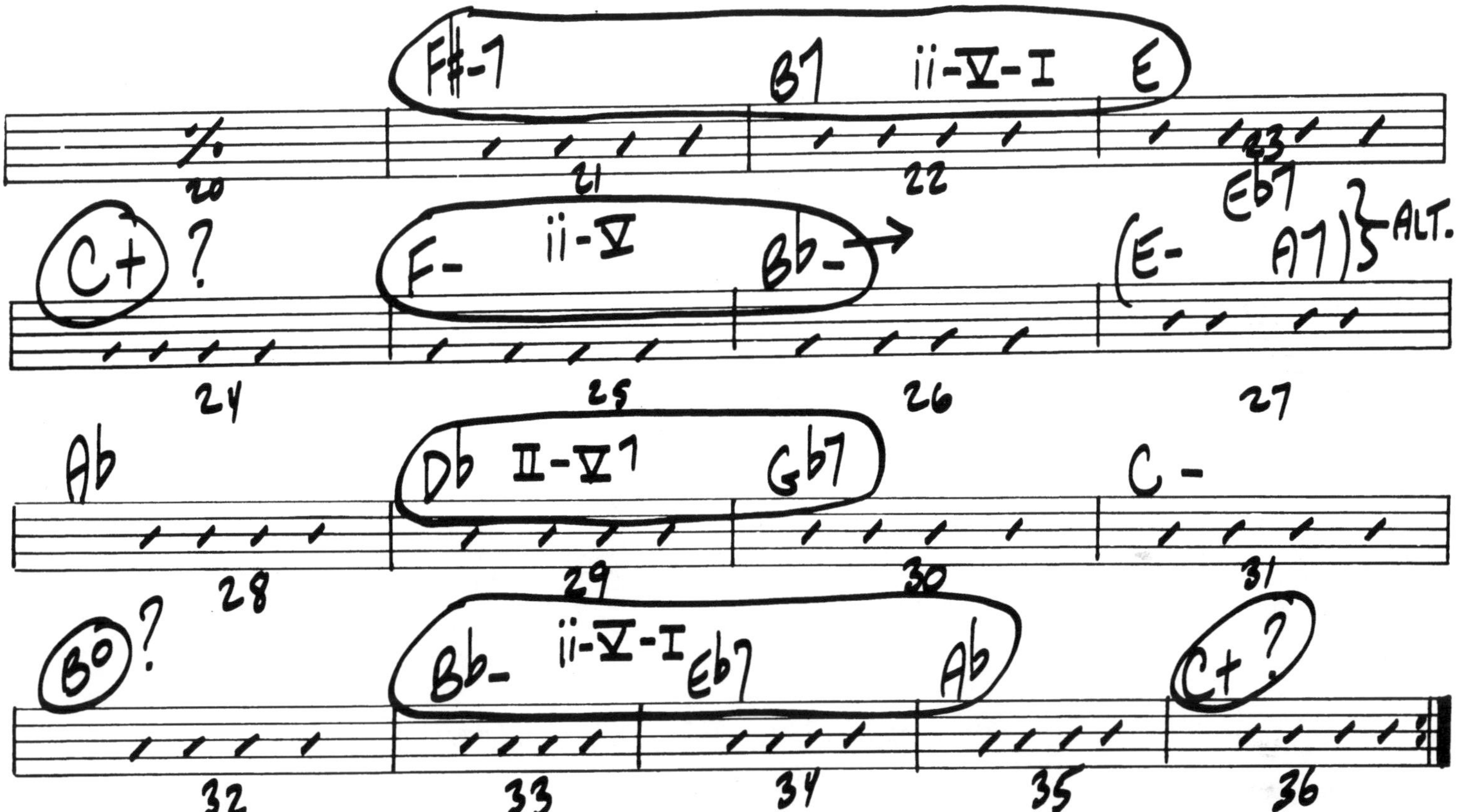

NOTE: C+ IN BARS 24 + 36 IS A SUB FOR C7. AUGMENTED IS USED BECAUSE MELODY NOTE IS A♭ OR G#. (B°) TO BE DISCUSSED LATER.

EXERCISE #19

TAKE THE FOLLOWING TUNE AND INSERT THE ALTERNATES IN PLACE OF THE CHORDS IN PARENTHESES. PLEASE NOTE REPEATS!

"WELL KNOWN" BE BOP TUNE

NOTE: BARS 9-14 ARE IDENTICAL TO BARS 1-8!

VOICINGS NOTE

There are many books available on how to voice your changes, so this book is purposely avoiding this issue. You must be aware, however, that in all of the material covered in this book, you must structure your chords properly for your harmony to sound good. Also, when altering a chord, you may use the information you have gotten here as a basis for constructing more complicated chords. In most cases, the melody will dictate how to structure your harmony. In the example below, observe the melody and how the accidentals are added to the basic chord.

EXAMPLE NO. 17 EXPLAINED.

BAR NO.	CHORD	ACCIDENTAL USED
1	dm	C- is the 7th of Dm
2	C7 b9	Db is the b9 of C7
3		NO ACCIDENTALS
4		NO ACCIDENTALS
5	Bb 6	G is the 6th of Bb
6	Bm	E is the 4th of B
7		NO ACCIDENTALS
8	D7b5	Ab is the b5 of D
9	G7#4	C# is the #4 of G
10	C7#9	Eb
		E or D# is the #9 of C7
		(note: in many cases you will see examples of incorrect accidentals, the reason being that many writers will use the most commonly seen note)
11	F major 7	E is the major 7th of F

At this point, you should try to find other examples of accidentals in your music and try to determine their use. Also, try to take tunes you already know and when changing the harmony, try to make your melody notes fit into your new changes as accidentals.

EXERCISE 20.

IDENTIFY THE FOLLOWING CHORDS.

EXAMPLES

HALF-DIMINISHED CHORDS

Tha half-diminished chord is notated by a circle with a slash through it (ϕ) or by stating it as a minor 7th chord with a flatted 5th (D–7♭5). You may choose to use it in place of any minor 7th chord providing the melody is not the 5th. See the below examples.

Note that in the above examples both forms of notation were used when substituting the half-diminished chord for the minor 7ths.

DIMINISHED CHORDS AS SUBSTITUTES FOR DOMINANT 7THS

The use of the diminished chord as a substitute for the dominant 7th chord is achieved in the following manner. First, determine where you are going. If, for example, you are resolving to an F chord, your normal choice would be the dominant C7. You may, however, select an E diminished chord. Now the E diminished is one-half step below your F or it is a major 3rd above your C7. Choose whatever means you like to determine the proper diminished chord substitute. Notice the examples below and then proceed to the next page and complete the exercises.

EX. #19

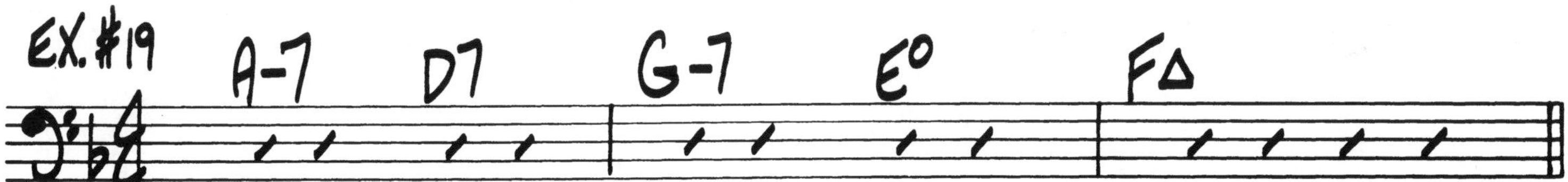

EX #19A

EXERCISES #21

A SUB. (ø) CHORDS FOR THE MINOR 7THS

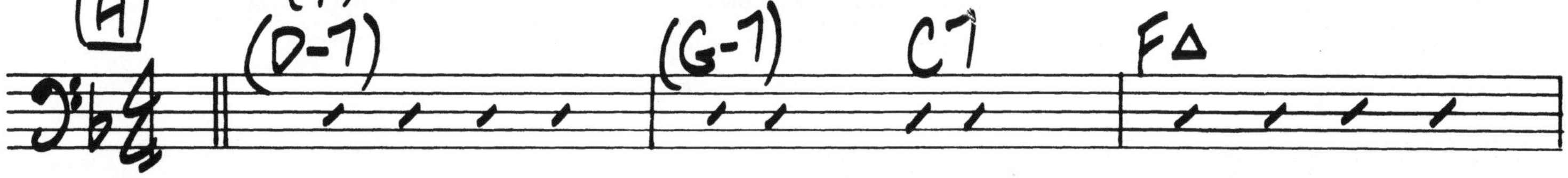

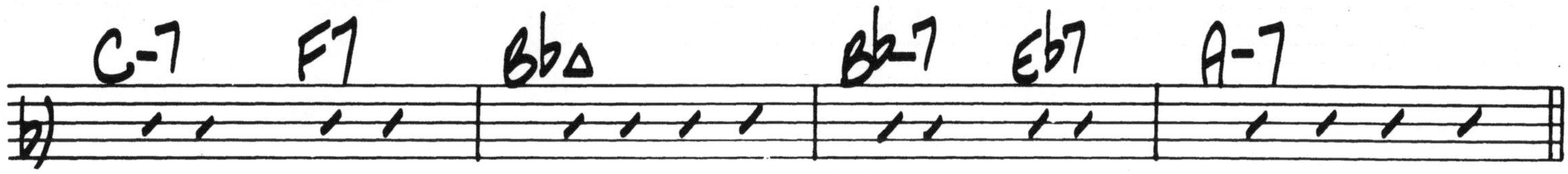

B SUB. (o) DIMINISHED CHORDS FOR THE DOM. 7THS

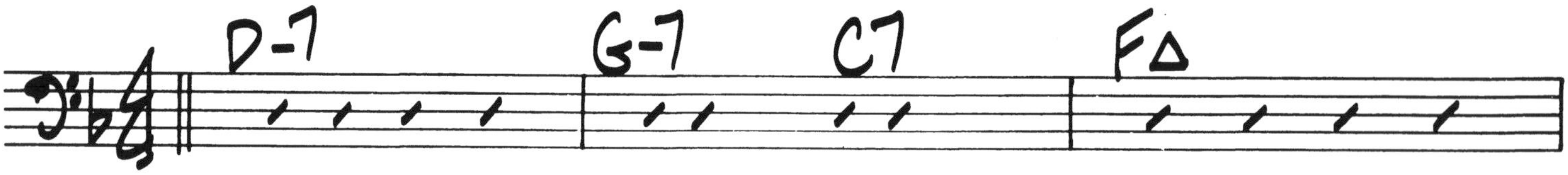

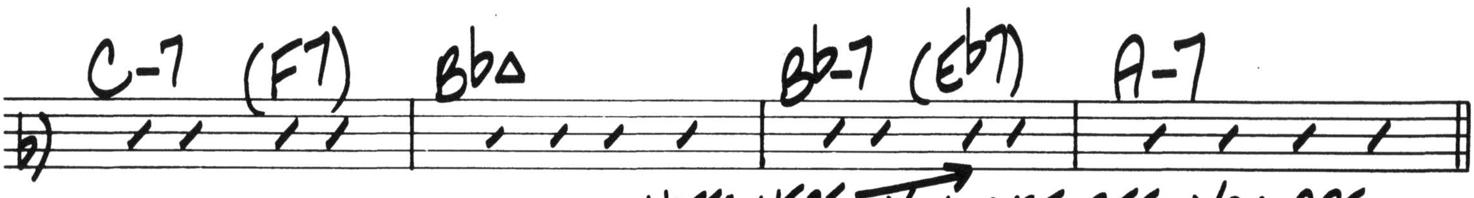

NOTE: HERE YOU MUST SEE YOU ARE GOING TO A-7.

C SUB. BOTH(ø) CHORDS AND (o) DIMINISHED CHORDS WHERE INDICATED

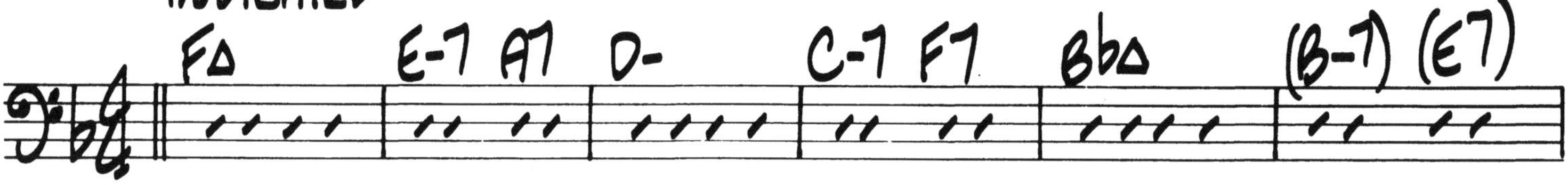

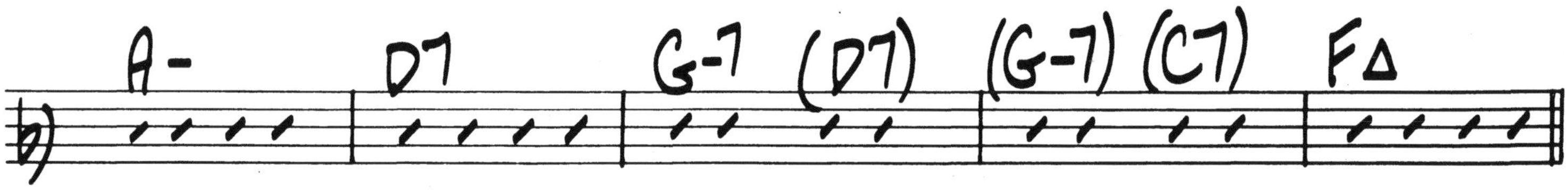

The remainder of this book is a series of exercises made from various tunes that are considered to be standards both in a commercial sense and as good Jazz tunes. It is the belief of this author that you, upon completion, will have a good solid basis from which to work in the future selection of chord progressions. If you are in doubt, please make references to the appropriate sections in this book. Below is an index to aid you.

#22 EXERCISES

SUPPLY THE NECESSARY TURNAROUNDS

BLUES #1

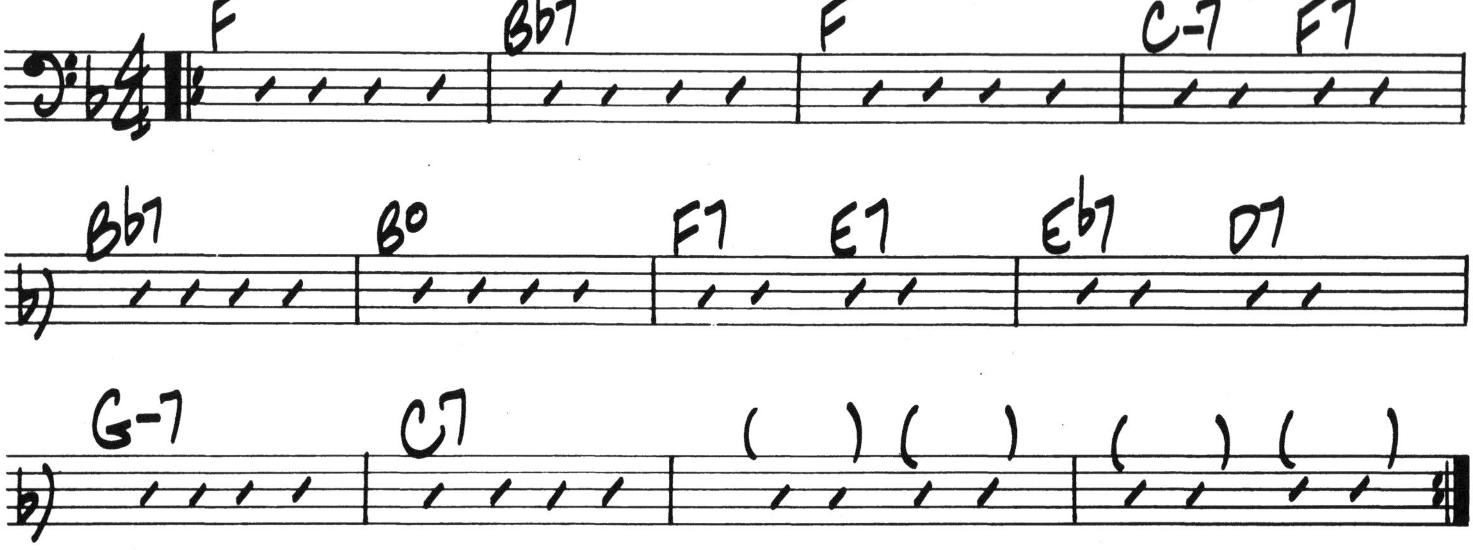

#23 COMPLETE THE EXTENSION OF THE CYCLE!

BLUES #2

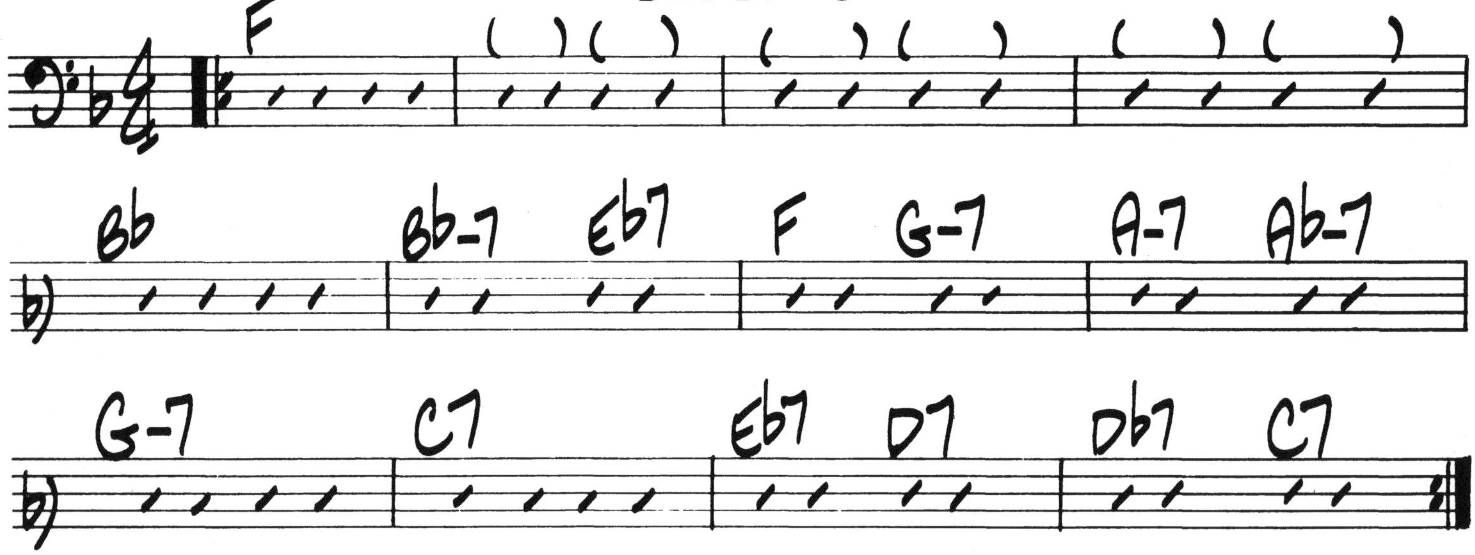

#24 SEE INSTRUCTIONS BELOW

— RHYTHM #1 —

INSTRUCTIONS

THE LAST 8 BARS ARE THE SAME AS THE FIRST 16 BARS. ALTER THE CHANGES BY USING THE <u>CYCLE EXTENSION</u> AND <u>THE ALTERNATE CYCLE</u>.

#25 INSTRUCTIONS AT BOTTOM OF PAGE

— TUNE #3 —

NOTE: COMPLETE THE TURN AROUND IN THE 1ST ENDING. COMPLETE THE CYCLE EXTENSION IN THE 2ND ENDING. YOU MAY CHOOSE THE ∅ WHERE IT APPLIES

COMPLETE THE CYCLE EXTENSION IN THE LAST 5 BARS. ANALYZE THE CHORDS IN PARATHESES. ALSO NOTE THE ii - V - I PROGRESSIONS.

#27

ANALYZE: ii - V - I

FIND ALTERNATES - FIND HALF DIMINISHED
FIND RELATIVE MINORS - FIND DIMINISHED
SUBSTITUTES.

#28

TUNE #5

IN BAR #4 – USE ii – V7 (ALTERNATE CYCLE)
" " #11 – USE CYCLE EXTENSION
" " #12 – USE ALTERNATE
" " #16 – USE ii7 – V7
" " #30 – USE ii7 – V (ALTERNATE CYCLE)

#29

TUNE #6

IN BAR #2 - SUB ALTERNATE
" " #3 - " "
" " #8 - USE ALTERNATE ALSO
" " #17 - USE V7
" " #18 - " "
" " #19 - USE ALTERNATE DOMINANT
" " #21 - USE ii7-V7
" " #23,24 - USE ALTERNATE ALSO

#80

— BALLAD #2 —

WHAT IS PROGRESSION IN BARS 1+2?
WHAT'S HAPPENING IN BARS 3+4?
WHAT DOES Bb7 IN BAR 7 SUB. FOR?
WHAT FUNCTION DOES Db7 IN BAR 8 TAKE?
" " " " " " 22 "
WHAT IS E7 IN BAR 23 TAKING THE PLACE OF?

#31 STUDY BLUES #1, HOW DOES MINOR BLUES DIFFER?

— MINOR BLUES #1 —

— MINOR BLUES #2 —

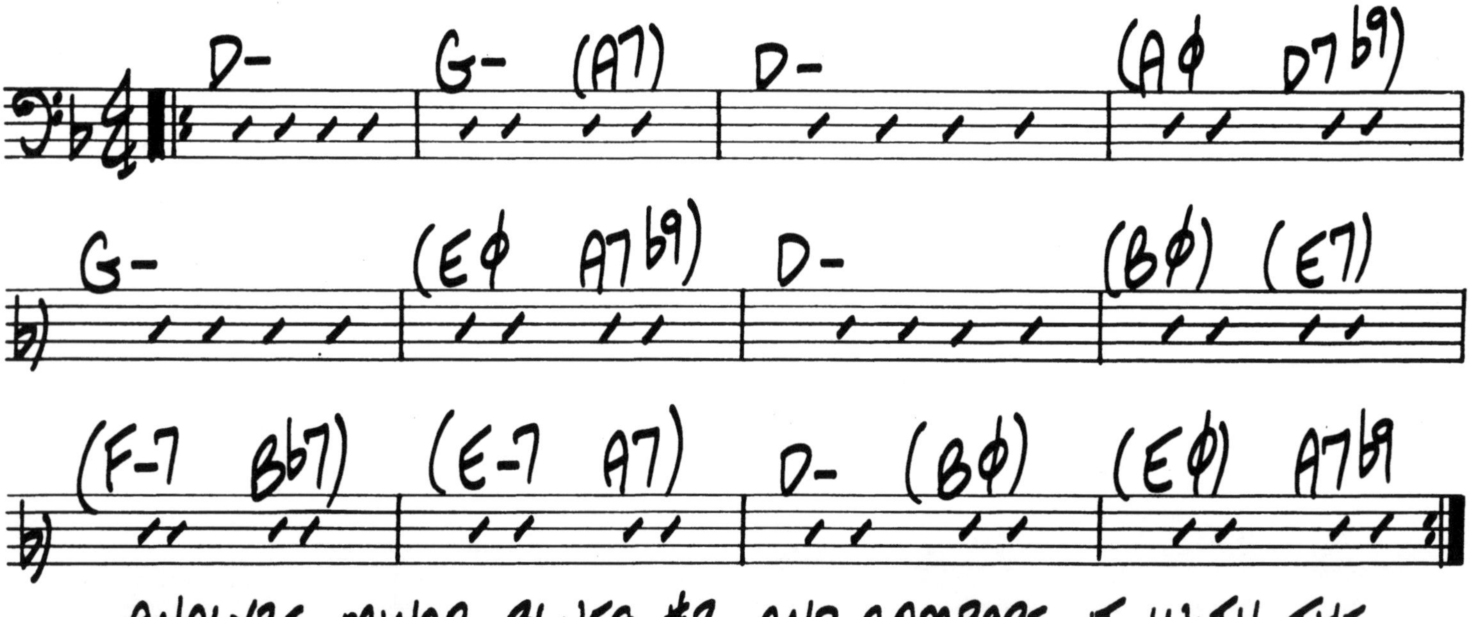

ANALYZE MINOR BLUES #2 AND COMPARE IT WITH THE MORE BASIC #1

FINAL NOTE

The exercises that you have just completed should be studied thoroughly and you should learn to play the tunes well because these are the changes to tunes that you will encounter time and again. You should also bear in mind that a technique for learning is precisely that and in no way should be used as a substitute for genuine improvisation.

Scales and chords are nothing more than a vocabulary from which you can choose when creating music. Refer to these techniques as if they were a dictionary. Also, continue to listen to other musicians, and hopefully, with your new observations in Jazz harmony, that which you may have found confusing in the past will disappear. Good luck.

Chuck Marohnic

NOTES